Original title:
Whispered in the Willows

Copyright © 2025 Creative Arts Management OÜ
All rights reserved.

Author: Riley Hawthorne
ISBN HARDBACK: 978-1-80567-402-3
ISBN PAPERBACK: 978-1-80567-701-7

Arcane Allusions of Autumn's Breath

Beneath the trees where squirrels play,
A tumbleweed rolls by in a fray,
The acorns fall in a nutty ballet,
As leaves dance around in a bright display.

A pumpkin with a grin so wide,
Hides a secret from the autumn tide,
He winks at crows upon the side,
As they caw and cackle, oh what a ride!

The winds blow whispers of lost parade,
Where every critter joins on parade,
With hats askew and itchy blades,
They march along, in mischief they wade.

A raccoon dons a scarf of red,
While dreaming of the pie he's fed,
With a twinkle of mischief in his head,
Oh autumn's breath, where laughter's spread!

So raise a toast with leaves in hand,
To the quirks and giggles of this land,
For in the rustle, we all understand,
Autumn's humor in nature's band.

Enchanted Dialogues at Dusk

The squirrels gossip about their snacks,
While leaves giggle with rustling quacks.
A raccoon offers wise old tales,
Of midnight feasts and grand old fails.

As moonlight spills like frozen cream,
The frogs croak out a quirky dream.
They trade jokes while crickets sing,
In that charm where laughter springs.

Breezes Carrying Ancient Echoes

The wind sways trees in cheeky jest,
Tickling branches, they dance their best.
A fox rolls over, thinks he's slick,
Shouting, 'Hey, who needs a stick?'

Hooting owls stumble through the dark,
Their puns hit soft, yet leave a mark.
With every gust, the humors rise,
In rustling leaves, a clownish guise.

Odes to the Overhanging Sky

Clouds puff up, donning silly hats,
While birds in lines engage in chats.
"Did you hear? The sun's on a spree!"
"I bet he's bingeing on golden tea."

Stars twinkle with a festive flair,
Joking, "Did you bring dessert to share?"
As night wears on, their laughter flows,
A cosmic show of cheeky prose.

Enigma of the Embossed Bark

Trees hold secrets, carved with care,
Whispering tales to none but air.
"Pass the bark! The punchline's near!"
Their stories tickle, drumming cheer.

Bugs join in, with tiny jokes,
A beetle cracks wise, amidst the pokes.
In nature's theater, laughter's grand,
Where punchlines bloom in a leafy band.

The Tone of Tranquil Trails

In shadows where the squirrels play,
A raccoon dances, bright and gay.
Leaves chuckle softly, winds do tease,
With grinning branches swaying in ease.

The path is lined with nature's glee,
A hedgehog winks 'neath a sprightly tree.
Birds gossip lightly in the air,
As laughter floats, with naught a care.

Rhythms of the Rooted Realm

Among the roots a secret tune,
The frogs form bands by the light of moon.
Crickets keep time in joyful throng,
While bees hum notes to their buzzing song.

A turtle dons his pirate hat,
And declares, "Let's dance!" with a little spat.
While butterflies join, flitting about,
In the rooted realm, there's never doubt.

Secrets in Stillness

Beneath the boughs, the frogs conspire,
With tales of mischief and wild fire.
An owl hoots jokes, wise and bright,
While shadows giggle, filled with delight.

The mossy stones have stories to tell,
Of sneaky vines that weave and swell.
A rabbit tries to juggle acorns,
As the moon snickers and slowly adorns.

Cadence of the Canopied Calm

The trees compose a melodious rhyme,
As squirrels plan their heist in prime.
Leaves shiver in laughter, a breezy jest,
While critters compete for the very best.

Beneath the canopy, where shadows spin,
A dance-off starts, let the games begin!
The laughter of nature fills the air,
In this lively world, free of care.

The Soft Pulse of Pine

In pines where squirrels scurry,
And chirps of birds get blurry,
A raccoon plays the flute,
While hedgehogs dance in a suit.

The breeze makes trees jiggle,
As bunnies bounce and giggle,
A deer spins like a top,
In nature's wacky shop.

Acorns drop like popcorn,
It's a party, not forlorn,
A beaver's doing the cha-cha,
While moles dance like a ballerina.

At dusk, the critters scheme,
To join the night's big dream,
Whispers float on the vine,
As night critters break into rhyme.

Melodies of the Meadow's Breath

In the fields where daisies smile,
Grasshoppers play marimbas with style,
A cat in a hat strums a tune,
While the cows prance like they're on the moon.

The butterflies twirl and spin,
They challenge the breeze for a win,
A worm pops up for a flash,
And with a grin, makes a splash.

Dandelions lip-sync along,
To the frogs' ribbiting song,
A caterpillar's doing the twist,
With friends who can't help but assist.

As twilight paints the sky with pink,
The meadow's creatures start to wink,
A symphony plays in such clever ways,
Making the night feel like a sunny daze.

Commanding Quiet of the Canopy

Under leaves, a secret choir,
Chirping crickets never tire,
A squirrel plots a silent heist,
While owls practice their advice.

Branches sway like dancers tall,
While shadows play hide and seek in the hall,
A raccoon tells vines a joke,
As a twig snaps, causing a yoke.

The woodpecker's rhythmic knock,
Makes the owls nod and rock,
Beneath the pines a mouse plays chess,
Unaware of the night's finesse.

In these woods, silence laughs loud,
With secrets tucked in every shroud,
Nature's comedy takes the stage,
In a forest of laughter for every age.

Sighs Beneath the Sunlit Leaf

In dappled light, squirrels conspire,
To steal naps and spark desire,
While lizards lounge and invent,
New games to distract from the bent.

A ladybug wears a tiny crown,
As mushrooms giggle, never frown,
The bees buzz in a jazzy beat,
While butterflies flutter on nimble feet.

The sun tickles the branches high,
While ants march in a silly line,
A toad croaks a haiku in jest,
While flowers laugh at the pest.

As the sun dips low in hues,
The forest whispers funny news,
With mirth beneath each verdant shell,
Nature's humor, casting its spell.

Hidden Voices of the Forest Floor

Amidst the leaves, a giggle sounds,
A squirrel juggles acorns around.
Rabbits dance in wild delight,
While crickets sing with all their might.

A badger's tale, a funny one,
He laughs at shadows, thinks it's fun.
The turtles play their version of chess,
In slow motion, they jest, I guess.

Mice tell jokes, a pun or two,
While fireflies glow a dazzling hue.
The owls hoot, they roll their eyes,
At antics below, a big surprise!

In the underbrush, the mischief grows,
Every creature wears a smile that glows.
Nature's stage, a lively show,
Where humor blooms and laughter flows.

Whispers among the Whispering Grass

In the meadow, grasses sway,
They share secrets, come what may.
Bumbles buzz with tales of flight,
While daisies giggle, pure delight.

A hedgehog steals a patch of sun,
With prickles proud, he thinks it fun.
Butterflies, in colors so bright,
Chase one another in sheer delight.

Caterpillars gossip on a leaf,
About the moths, who won't believe.
The playful breeze adds a little flair,
Laughing softly without a care.

In this grassy world of mirth,
Each blade's a witness to their worth.
Nature's laughter fills the air,
A joyous concert everywhere.

Tales Told by the Twisting Roots

Beneath the bark, the roots entwine,
They share their tales, both silly and fine.
A fox, with swagger, struts about,
While trees lie back, grinning, no doubt.

Above the ground, a curious sight,
A raccoon dons a mask at night.
The mushrooms giggle, "What a show!"
As laughter sprouts in the earth below.

A tortoise grumbles, "I'm not slow,"
While bouncing beetles steal the show.
Every twist and turn they take,
Leaves tales of laughter in their wake.

Roots wrap around their funny lore,
Ever growing, wanting more.
In the soil where stories play,
Humor dances, come what may.

Gentle Songs of the Sylvan Shadows

In the cool dusk, shadows sway,
Trees tell tales at the end of day.
A raccoon sings in silly tones,
While owls chuckle in their homes.

The brook babbles, jokes it shares,
With splashes bright, it ruffles airs.
Fireflies giggle in the dark,
As crickets chirp a joyful spark.

Bats swoop low, with comic grace,
Making faces, a merry race.
Even the moon wears a smile,
As creatures amuse for a while.

Among the trees, where shadows blend,
Laughter echoes, without end.
In the twilight, where dreams reside,
Nature's humor, our joyful guide.

Rustling Reminders of Repose

In a grove where breezes play,
Leaves giggle as they sway.
Squirrels dance from branch to branch,
Rabbits join in a leafy ranch.

Sunlight peeks through fluffy clouds,
Tickling noses of the crowds.
The trees wear hats of bright green cheer,
And even grumpy owls seem to leer.

Vines tell tales of secret games,
Of playful winds that tease names.
With twirls and swirls, the shadows wink,
While frogs toadally link and blink.

So grab a seat on the grass so soft,
And let your laughter soar aloft.
Nature's jesters, wild and free,
Dancing 'neath the old oak tree.

Decrypted Lyrics in the Landscape

The daisies hum a silly tune,
While chipmunks tap to the afternoon.
Clouds shaped like snacks float overhead,
Peanut butter dreams in the sky, spread.

In the meadows, cows strike a pose,
While frogs croak out their secret prose.
A butterfly flutters with a wink,
Inviting all to pause and think.

Blades of grass wear tiny hats,
Chasing echoing giggles of chats.
The butterflies learn to tango and sway,
Dancing until the close of day.

Nature's antics never cease,
Whimsical scenes that bring us peace.
So hum along with the world so bright,
And let your spirit take to flight.

The Silence Between the Stars

Twinkling lights play hide and seek,
While crickets chirp, their nightly peak.
The moon wears shades and winks at me,
As if to share a cosmic spree.

A comet sneezes across the night,
And giggles escape from the satellite.
Constellations draw out comic strips,
As astronauts juggle with moonlight tips.

The Milky Way spills secrets untold,
Of stardust tales, both brave and bold.
While shooting stars dive and twirl,
Dancing with laughter in cosmic swirl.

So look up high, and you might find,
The universe's quirky, playful mind.
Let the silence between the stars ring,
Where even the night sky loves to sing.

Notes from a Nesting Nightingale

In a cozy nook, a nightingale sings,
Dropping notes like joyful flings.
With every chirp, the trees jiggle,
And all around, the fireflies giggle.

Her nest is a palace, fluff and cheer,
With tiny trinkets, gathered near.
Peeking in, I see a sock,
A shiny button — she's quite the rock!

The morning light beams, bright and spry,
While grumpy insects buzz nearby.
But she just twirls, not one care to spare,
And fills the air with melodies rare.

So let her serenade your day,
As you sway along in a light-hearted way.
For in her song, we find delight,
A joyful tune that feels just right.

Heartbeats of the Hushed Woods

In the quiet woods where shadows play,
The squirrels gather, plotting the day.
They toss acorns like tiny grenades,
While the owls hoot in amused charades.

A rabbit hops on a rogue twig,
Spraining its ankle, oh what a gig!
The deer chuckle, shaking their heads,
As the rabbit whines, fluffing its beds.

Trees tremble with laughter, roots shake with glee,
As frogs croak in beat, like musicians carefree.
The light dances through leaves in delight,
Shiny beetles join in, shining bright.

With each breeze, the forest teases,
Nature's comedy, it never ceases.
As all creatures join in this merry jest,
The heartbeats of woods, truly the best!

Glimmers in the Greenery

Through the foliage, sparkles fly,
Fireflies battling under the sky.
They zip and zoom, a merry race,
While the butterflies laugh, just in case.

The beetles boast of their shiny bling,
While ants march in, a jesting fling.
"We're the true stars of this night show!"
They shout in unison, putting on a glow.

A raccoon sings with a comical tone,
Claiming he's king without a throne.
The trees sway, joining his tune,
Under the watch of the watching moon.

In this realm of laughter and light,
Glimmers dance in whimsical sight.
For in the greenery, joy takes flight,
Nature's own theater, pure delight!

Tales from the Twisted Twigs

On twisted twigs, tall tales entwine,
Of owls that waltz and porcupines that dine.
A fox in a hat plays chess with a goat,
While sneaky raccoons take notes in a boat.

Each branch holds secrets, silly and bold,
From squirrels who scamper, to stories retold.
A turtle with glasses, wise as can be,
Claims he's the smartest in all of the spree.

A chorus of critters, each with their part,
The forest's own band, a laugh-filled art.
With every strange tale, the laughter grows,
In this enchanted realm where playfulness flows.

So gather round, for a twist and a cheer,
The forest's wild tales are far more than sheer.
In the hub of the twists, where all creatures dig,
The merriment lives, oh so big!

Soft Footfalls of the Forest

With soft footfalls, the critters creep,
Tiptoeing gently, not making a peep.
But then a branch snaps, oh what a sound,
A dance party starts, all around.

The hedgehogs roll in a flurry of fun,
While the bunnies hop, until daylight is done.
A drum made of logs, they thump and they thud,
A waltz in the wild, a comical flood.

Each rustle and giggle echoes with glee,
As if the trees also join in the spree.
The air fills with chuckles from here to the sky,
As crickets chirp notes that never say die.

So hear the soft footfalls, a symphonic cheer,
In this jolly forest, with friends far and near.
Where the fun never stops and laughter prevails,
In the dance of the wild, where joy never fails!

The Murmur of Mellow Moons

In the night, a raccoon sneaks,
Chasing shadows with silly squeaks.
Stars chuckle at the sight they see,
As playful owls giggle in glee.

A fox in a scarf struts with pride,
Prowling where mischief does abide.
Every leaf whispers a silly tune,
Under the gaze of a grinning moon.

Bunnies leap in a hopscotch race,
Stomping softly, no time to trace.
Each thump echoes the laughter bright,
Chasing fireflies, they spark the night.

Skunks start to salsa, tail in the air,
While turtles groove without a care.
Nature's a stage with the softest jest,
Where even the grass feels its very best.

Nature's Softest Promises

In the garden, flowers wear a grin,
Petals converse, 'Shall we let the fun begin?'
Bees buzz in rhythm, telling tales,
Of nectar quests and swirling gales.

Each breeze carries a secret laugh,
As squirrels plot their nutty gaff.
Joy dances lightly on the streams,
While frogs croak in outlandish dreams.

Ladybugs waddle in a parade,
Creating mischief, none will evade.
With a flutter, they chase light around,
Nature's giggle is the sweetest sound.

The sun peeks through the clouds aglow,
Tickling leaves to join in the show.
Nature's soft promises weave and twirl,
In a world bustling with a cheeky whirl.

Laughter Dancing on Drifting Winds

The wind teases branches with a light heart,
Tickling whispers, a mischievous art.
Clouds chuckle as they float above,
Carrying giggles like a gentle shove.

With each rustle, the world takes a chance,
A deer prances like it's a ballet dance.
Crickets chirp a serenade so sweet,
As frogs find rhythm in tapping feet.

Grasshoppers spring with bounce and flair,
Wearing tiny socks, they dance in the air.
Nature's laughter, a wild, sweet breeze,
Tickles the trees, puts all minds at ease.

In this arena where lighthearted roams,
Every chirp welcomes joyful homes.
The day's waltz is a playful spin,
While laughter pirouettes on drifting wind.

The Solace of Subtle Sounds

In the hush of dusk, crickets commence,
A symphony echoes, it's quite intense.
Whispers of grass tell stories anew,
Mice giggle softly, 'It's just me and you.'

The moon hums a tune to the rolling hills,
While owls join in with their nighttime thrills.
Each rustle carries a joke or two,
As fireflies flicker, like stars that flew.

Dewdrops chuckle on petals so bright,
Singing sweet secrets under moonlight.
A lullaby weaves through the trees vast,
Comedic whispers of nature amassed.

The night enfolds in its cozy wrap,
With branches swaying in a comical tap.
In nature's arms, all worries stay bound,
Within the solace of subtle sounds.

Echoes Beneath the Boughs

In the shade a squirrel leaps,
Chasing shadows, taking peeks.
The branches giggle, oh so sly,
While acorns fall and pigeons fly.

A raccoon wears a leaf like a hat,
It struts around, thinking it's flat.
The oak tree chuckles, rings with mirth,
Nature's jesters dance with worth.

A singing frog, a croaking tune,
While fireflies light up like the moon.
With every hop and every cheer,
The woods are full of jpegs dear.

So come along, let laughter swell,
In the green where tales do dwell.
No need for gloom, just join the rove,
And share the laughs that nature wove.

Secrets of the Silent Grove

Beneath the leaves the rabbits race,
With twitching noses, each a face.
They trip on roots and tumble down,
While the fox watches without a frown.

An owl hoots, a clown on a branch,
Making faces, not a bit brash.
The turtles laugh as they slowly tease,
"Catch us if you can, if you please!"

A family of deer strike awkward poses,
While the elder crow plays with roses.
The chuckles rise among the trees,
As everyone tries to bring to knees.

With every rustle, a giggle grows,
In the cracks of laughter, wisdom flows.
Nature's fiesta, a secret show,
In the grove where merriment glows.

Murmurs of the Moonlit Woods

By night the woods come alive with cheer,
The owls debate, 'Who's the best here?'
The raccoons play cards with the stars,
While shadows shuffle, hiding their scars.

A laughing brook spills over stones,
As frogs compete in their nutty tones.
With glowworms twinkling like wild dreams,
They join the fun with ribbiting themes.

The moon winks down, a watchful friend,
As fireflies dance, a dazzling blend.
Each branch holds tales, each leaf a grin,
In this merry world, let the jokes begin.

So gather 'round, let the night unfold,
With every laugh, a tale retold.
In this glow, the woods unveil,
The humor woven like moonlit veil.

Songs of the Shivering Leaves

Leaves rustle softly, singing a song,
Of chipmunks scurrying all day long.
They tumble and roll in nature's spree,
While they gossip about the old oak tree.

A spider spins a web so bright,
While debating if it's left or right.
Everyone chuckles at the spectacle made,
In this lively place where jokes won't fade.

The wind tells tales, a mischievous breeze,
Tickles the branches, makes them sneeze.
It's a concert of giggles, a dance in the air,
With laughter cascading everywhere.

So listen close to the playful sounds,
In this realm where humor abounds.
For in every rustle, a joke is tossed,
In the foliage where fun is never lost.

Reflections in the Leafy Silence

In the quiet glade where the squirrels dance,
A chipmunk twirls in a froggy trance.
The trees giggle softly, leaves all askew,
As nature discusses what pranks they will do.

A rabbit comes hopping, a hat on his head,
He claims he's a magician, but he's really misread.
The branches are chuckling, the sun's in a fit,
While shadows roll over trying not to split.

The breeze tells a joke, the flowers all blush,
A bee buzzes in with a very loud hush.
Oh, laughter erupts from the thicket so wide,
Where daisies and daisies take giggles in stride.

And underneath the oak, the laughter won't cease,
With each little rustle, they're plotting for peace.
But what kind of truce can the critters create?
In this leafy silence, it's all about fate.

Breath of the Boundless Breach

A tortoise in shades is skating on grass,
While weeds hold a party, folks say it's a gas.
The wind starts to whistle a peculiar tune,
As the frogs and the crickets begin to festoon.

A dance-off erupts between bee and ant,
With everyone cheering, well, as much as they can.
The mole's got a trumpet, he's ready to play,
While the owls keep time, nodding heads in array.

Cartwheeling fireflies light up the night,
With giggles and grins, they've taken to flight.
The hedgehogs are snickering at each little blunder,
As catfish flip fins, making waves of pure wonder.

Oh, come join the fun, in this magical patch,
Where laughter is caught in a bubbling snatch.
So heed not the murmur of clouds rolling by,
Just dance in the breach, let your spirit fly high.

Secrets of the Soothing Shade

Under the giants, secrets do bloom,
A spider tells tales inside of her room.
With whispers of squirrels and shadows of chat,
They gossip of mischief, like where lies the cat.

The sun filters down like a warming surprise,
While the flowers all giggle with fluttering sighs.
A dandelion claims he's the funniest sprout,
But the daisies just snicker, they know what he's about.

A picnic's been set with the ants on parade,
As they steal from the spread, their plans all laid.
With sandwiches flying and laughter so loud,
The creatures come forth, both silly and proud.

So, stroll through the shade, where the secrets are smooth,
Where the trees swap their gossip and critters all groove.
In the soothing shadows, the world feels just right,
With laughter and antics that dance through the night.

Enchantment of the Emerald Enclave

In the heart of the glen, where the green things collide,
A dragonfly boasts he can dance on the tide.
With his wings all aflutter, he spins with delight,
While the frogs sit amused in their formal attire.

The ferns sway and chuckle, they're in on the fun,
As a gopher named Gerald races past on the run.
With a tutu of petals and a tale to unfold,
He claims he can fly, if only he's bold.

The sun sets in laughter, splitting cheeks in the dusk,
Decorating the smiles in a shimmer of musk.
The night creatures wonder what antics may flare,
As the fireflies twinkle, a festive affair.

So gather your buddies, bring snacks and your cheer,
Join the enchantment, don't hold back your jeer.
For in this emerald enclave, joy reigns so bright,
Where silliness lives and laughter takes flight.

Riddles of the Rustic Retreat

In a cabin deep in the woods,
A raccoon found our snacks,
He wore a tiny hat, you see,
And danced like he had a knack.

The squirrels held a talent show,
With acorns as their prize,
But one fell flat while telling jokes,
His friends rolled their small eyes.

The fireflies joined in the fun,
With flickers and silly flights,
They lit the stage with a glowing cheer,
As crickets cheered with delight.

In the heart of nature's jest,
Where laughter fills the air,
The woods become a funny fest,
In every nook and layer.

Tones of Timeless Tranquility

In a field of daisies bright,
A goat wore glasses wide,
He tried to read the plants around,
But the grass just laughed and lied.

A turtle in a sunlit glade,
Claimed he could run the race,
Then took a nap, right in the shade,
For victory's a slower pace.

The butterflies began to tease,
With paint upon their wings,
While frogs played jazz on lily pads,
And hummed of joyous things.

In the stillness, joy is found,
In nature's playful prance,
The laughter loops—a merry sound,
In every fleeting glance.

Glimpses of Gossamer Dreams

A spider spun a silken tale,
Of mice who wore high shoes,
They danced upon a moonlit veil,
With steps that made us snooze.

The owls in wisdom gave a hoot,
But tripped on their own wings,
As raccoons played a game of flute,
And sang of silly things.

The stars twinkled, laughing bright,
At shadows on the ground,
While fireflies juggled through the night,
In frolics all around.

In dreams where whimsy holds the reign,
And laughter paints the skies,
The forest sways, a sweet refrain,
As joy in spirit flies.

Echoed Memories in the Elm

Beneath the elm, the tales unfold,
Of turtles making pies,
With ingredients pure and bold,
Yet the flavor made them sighs.

A squirrel donned a chef's tall hat,
And mixed nuts with great flair,
But when he tasted, went 'Oh rat!',
His foul concoction, rare!

The birds held court on branches high,
Debating what to wear,
Feathers bright or dull and shy,
They fluffed with utmost care.

In the shade where giggles spin,
And memories come alive,
The laughter echoes deep within,
As nature starts to thrive.

Nightfall in the Noble Woods

As dusk descends with a quirky cheer,
Squirrels hold a nutty auction near.
Owls hoot softly, gossip on the breeze,
While crickets serenade, trying to tease.

The raccoons plan a midnight feast,
Beneath the stars, their joy increased.
A fox struts by in a dapper hat,
Declaring himself the forest's aristocrat.

The fireflies dance in a flickering show,
Chatting about who's the best dancer to know.
An elusive deer joins the merry band,
Swapping silly tales of life close at hand.

As laughter peals through the leafy dome,
Creatures of the night call this place home.
With smiles lit bright on their furry faces,
Together they bask in nature's embraces.

Flickering Flames of the Ferns

In a glade where shadows spin and sway,
The ferns giggle as the campfire plays.
Marshmallows roast, a sticky affair,
While critters compete for the sweetest share.

A badger tells tales, his voice full of flair,
Claiming he once did a flip through the air.
But the raccoons roll eyes, they've seen him fall,
When skimming across that old creek wall.

The owls hoot 'round and thump their wings,
Offering wisdom on the wildest things.
"Do socks really match? Should we care?" they muse,
As the breeze carries scents of last night's stews.

Laughter erupts, like the sparks that fly,
Creatures unite 'neath the ink-black sky.
With friendship alight, they shout and they cheer,
Celebrating the moments, the funny, the dear.

Conversations with the Ancient Oaks

In a corner where giants stand tall and wise,
Squirrels chat on branches, making up lies.
"Did you see that woodpecker?" one starts to say,
"Drumming so loud, he scared the sun away!"

The oaks just chuckle, their leaves softly quiver,
"Kids these days, oh, how they do deliver!"
They share stories of storms when they danced with the breeze,
And how leafy gossip brings everyone to tease.

A timid turtle sneaks in, a bit shy,
"I swear I saw a dandelion fly.
It gave me a wink and then burst into fluff,
I thought I'd shout, but I just didn't have the stuff!"

The oaks reply, "Oh, sweet little one,
In this world of wonders, that's just so fun!"
As laughter echoes through the vast green sea,
The wisdom of trees mixes with humor, carefree.

Whispers of the Winding Trails

Along the path where mischief aligns,
A squirrel takes bets on some daring climbs.
"I'll leap to that branch!" he proudly declares,
"We'll toast to my skills, so brave, so rare!"

But a nearby rabbit rolls his big eyes wide,
"I've seen you trip on that vine last slide!"
Yet with a pep, the squirrel bounds ahead,
Leaving critics laughing, full of good dread.

Tales are exchanged of mishaps and tunes,
Among ants and beetles and the shy raccoons.
A butterfly flutters, gossiping bright,
"Who made the flower blush pink with delight?"

With each twist and turn, the stories unfold,
Of silly creatures that dare to be bold.
In this lively lane, where humor prevails,
Nature's comedy unfolds on the trails.

Traces of Forgotten Stories

Beneath a tree, a squirrel knits,
Dreams of acorns, and some misfits.
With tiny paws, it makes a scene,
   Life's a nutty, zany dream!

The breeze chuckles, tickling leaves,
Old tales dance, as daylight weaves.
A raccoon grins, oh what a sight,
   In shadows, laughter takes flight.

Mice hold meetings, plotting plans,
While ants march on in tiny bands.
What snacks to steal, they all agree,
   A buffet feast of crumbs and glee!

So here we sit, with giggles shared,
In nature's chaos, none are scared.
Each rustling leaf, a joke or pun,
   In forest fun, we've just begun!

Swaying Souls in the Shade

Beneath the canopy, a joke is spun,
As shadows groan and sunlight runs.
A frog croaks loud, with comedic flair,
While grasshoppers leap through the air.

The daisies giggle, swaying in place,
While sunbeams dance with a wacky grace.
A sleepy snail, with dreams of speed,
Sighs softly, wishing for a steed.

The owl winks, a midnight clown,
While the crickets chirp a silly sound.
Together they sing in harmonious rhyme,
As twilight melts into silly time.

In the shade of the trees, all's merry and bright,
Where laughter is gold, and joy takes flight.
Each giggling leaf shares the day's delight,
Throughout the woods, every heart feels light!

The Dance of Delicate Foliage

Leaves sway lightly, wearing crowns of green,
Twisting and turning, a leafy routine.
The wind's a prankster, blowing just right,
Causing branches to giggle with delight.

A butterfly flutters, winks at the sun,
While beetles shake it, oh what fun!
Together they burst into silly prance,
In nature's theater, they all take a chance.

A squirrel in a tutu makes quite the scene,
Dancing on branches, not a care, so keen.
The whole glen chuckles, a sight to behold,
As whispers of joy in the leaves unfold.

In the theater of woods, where laughter's the lead,
Foliage dances, planting a seed.
Of silliness, laughter, each creature's role,
In the show of the trees, the heart finds its goal!

Soft Serenades in the Glade

In the glade where shadows play,
A rabbit tells a joke today.
"Mice can't dance!" it hops and beams,
While beetles giggle in silly dreams.

A gentle breeze brings whispers low,
Of antics held in gardens' glow.
The daisies curtsy, with chuckles and cheer,
While tiny ants stand up to jeer.

The woodpecker drums a comical beat,
As frogs crack up at the rhythm's feat.
Nature's orchestra finds its groove,
In every note, the heart must move.

Between the trees, the laughter lifts,
Creating joy, nature's gifts.
So gather near, let giggles parade,
In the sweet serenades of the glade!

Flickers of Light Through Leafy Lattice

Sunbeams dance like eager mice,
Twiddling tails with a hint of spice.
Leaves clap hands in a leafy delight,
As shadows play, oh what a sight!

Squirrels chatter with gossiping glee,
Accusing the birds of tampering free.
Laughter rings from trunk to vine,
Nature is jesting, oh how divine!

A rabbit hops in a jolly dash,
While crickets croon a hap-hap-hash.
Together they weave a zany parade,
Beneath the green, where joy is displayed!

Even the breeze can't hold its cheer,
Tickling the grass, spreading the smear.
It bends and bows with mirthful zest,
In this wood of giggles, all are blessed!

Beneath the Blossoming Canopy.

Petals tumble in a sweet ballet,
Dancing around, come what may.
A nose tickled by fragrant tease,
As a bumblebee drops in with ease.

Giggling flowers all in a row,
Compete for the sun, putting on a show.
The chatter of bees fills the air,
"Who's the fairest?" they buzz with flair!

Butterflies flutter in wild debate,
Over who's got the best garden plate.
Pansies blush and daisies sigh,
While forget-me-nots wink, "Oh me, oh my!"

A squirrel's jest, a loud, silly shout,
Rattles the buds as he runs about.
Nature's folly, a cheeky spree,
Under this canopy, wild and free!

Echoes Beneath the Boughs

Beneath the branches, secrets sway,
The echoes of laughter in playful array.
Nature giggles with a rustling sound,
While critters scurry all around.

A raccoon sneezes, adds to the fun,
Leaves chuckle softly, "Oh what a pun!"
With shadows dancing, each step a jest,
In their playful realm, they feel blessed.

Frogs croak jokes in a ribbiting tone,
While turtles nod in laughter well-known.
The sun joins in with a warm, bright grin,
As nature's theater begins to spin!

Every branch teems with stories untold,
In this woodland, where laughter is bold.
The echoes of glee strengthen the bond,
As nature plays on, and we respond!

Secrets Cradled by the Breeze

The breeze carries whispers, playful yet sly,
Tickling the leaves as it woos by.
A fox tells tales of mischief too,
To the treetops swaying in the blue.

Each gust sprinkles laughter like fairy dust,
Sending sunlight and shadows in a whimsical trust.
A wiggly worm shares jokes with a snail,
While the robin chimes in, hearty and hail!

Rabbits hop and tumble with grace,
Each thump and giggle is a wild race.
Under the sky, they dance and tease,
In a world where joy is carried with ease!

So let us revel in nature's high jinks,
With giggles and wiggles, not a moment to think.
For the breeze cradles secrets in playful repose,
In this lively glade where humor just grows!

The Lure of Leafy Lores

Beneath the trees, a squirrel pranced,
Chasing shadows, he danced,
A rogue acorn, his prize in hand,
He's king of the leafy land.

The branches chuckle, leaves all sway,
As critters plot their silly play,
With every scamper, every dive,
The forest hums, alive, alive!

A rabbit leaps with handy flair,
While finding a welcoming lair,
A thicket's maze brings laughter near,
In nature's whim, we shed a tear.

So gather 'round and take a seat,
These leafy tales can't be beat,
For in the woods, where oddballs meet,
Life's tiny quirks are fresh and sweet.

Quiet Revelations in the Thicket

In shady spots, the sunlight plays,
Where leafy whispers start their praise,
A butterfly in polka dots,
Is gossiping with all the tots.

The frogs in chorus croak a tune,
While crickets harmonize at noon,
With every note, the laughter grows,
In secret places, joy just flows.

A raccoon dons a top hat grand,
Pretending to be quite the band,
The owls roll eyes, they know the score,
It's just another show before.

Sweet moments nestled, soft and slight,
In woodland revels, pure delight,
So listen close, let laughter chime,
In thickets where the fun beats time.

Dancing Light and Silent Tones

Beneath the boughs, the shadows twirl,
As fireflies spin, their lights unfurl,
A beetle boogies, just for fun,
While flowers sway, all on the run.

The sun dips low in golden glow,
While murmurs of the night winds blow,
The moon rolls in, a cheeky chap,
In nature's dance, there's no mishap.

A giggling breeze does play, oh look!
As ants form circles, read their book,
The pagination's off, you see,
Who knew the woods were jubilee?

So come and join this vibrant scene,
The light and laughter, pure and keen,
In every nook, find joy and grace,
In nature's dance, we find our place.

Secrets Flowing with the Stream

A babbling brook reveals some lore,
With splashes bright, it starts to score,
The gossip flies as fish do leap,
They share their secrets, run and creep.

In pools of dreams, the otters sing,
Of silly things the summer brings,
A turtle joins in with a grin,
Who knew the stream had such a spin?

With every ripple, fun takes flight,
The frisky frogs croak late at night,
The stones, they chuckle, tales abound,
In nature's realm, where joy is found.

So wade along, let laughter seep,
In watery worlds, the memories keep,
With every splash, a giggle schemes,
For secrets flow like wildest dreams.

Stories Born from the Foliage

In the shade where squirrels chat,
And raccoons wear hats so fat,
A tree trunk tells a joke or two,
While leaves giggle, how about you?

The breeze carries tales afar,
Of a cat who dreams of a car.
A frog sings opera by a stream,
While the sunbeams dance like a dream.

The owls high up try to rhyme,
With crickets keeping perfect time.
Ants march on in their parade,
While grasshoppers play serenade.

Among the roots, the fun goes round,
With mushrooms giggling underground.
Each rustle shares a silly tease,
As laughter sweeps through the trees.

Enchanted Tone of the Timber

The branches sway with giggling hues,
Each leaf a tiny, whispered muse.
A squirrel tells a fandango tale,
While beetles march with wings to sail.

The trees are full of secret schemes,
Where shadows play with silly dreams.
A hedgehog rolls in grass so tall,
And mushrooms wave, "Come one, come all!"

When the sun dips low, the fun's not done,
For foxes join in on the run.
They prance and leap in moonlit ballet,
As nightingales sing to end the day.

Each crackling twig has something to share,
With echoes floating in the air.
What laughter sprouts from roots and bows,
When nature itself can't help but espouse.

Twilight Reflections Among the Trees

As shadows stretch and branches yawn,
The creatures gather at the dawn.
A raccoon shares his dinner plans,
While fireflies buzz like tiny fans.

The moon peeks through, a playful tease,
Tickling leaves held by a gentle breeze.
A hedgehog wearing tiny shoes,
Makes leaps and bounds like he could cruise.

The owls' wisdom is quite absurd,
For every thought's a tiny bird.
Chasing giggles from branch to ground,
In bubbling laughter, joy is found.

So gather round, you roots so dear,
Let's spin a yarn, let's shed a tear.
For in this forest, we're all in on it,
The tales we weave, they surely fit.

Whirl of Wind-Whipped Words

In the canopy, a tempest plays,
Whirling whispers turn into phrase.
A cicada buzzes with things to say,
While curls of vapor dance and sway.

The pine trees laugh with crafty schemes,
Swapping secrets in sunlit beams.
Rabbits hop with comedic flair,
In a race, they're floating on air.

With bushes holding giggling boughs,
And twirling dandelions in rows,
The whole glade joins in on the jest,
While everything joins in with zest.

As soft winds blow a merry tune,
The night blooms bright with a glowing moon.
Each rustling leaf is a newfound cheer,
As earthworms giggle, "We're all here!"

A Diary of Dappled Light

In shades of green, the squirrels play,
They steal my snacks without delay.
A dance of leaves, a cheeky sight,
The sunbeams laugh; oh, what a delight!

Adventures made in quiet nooks,
They turn my pages, no need for books.
A butterfly flits with a silly grace,
Even the mushrooms wear a smiley face!

The brook hums tunes of jest and cheer,
While ants line up, 'What's for dinner here?'
And as I chuckle at their parade,
The shadows gather, the games are played!

So here's a tale of sunlit schemes,
Where giggles twinkle in golden beams.
With a notebook poised in this leafy glen,
I'll write of fun; let the laughter begin!

Nature's Concert of Cadence

The crickets chirp a jolly song,
While flowers sway, they can't go wrong.
A symphony of rustling leaves,
Even the bumblebees wear their sleeves!

The wind shakes hands with all it meets,
As drummers pound with tiny feet.
A frog hops by, an off-key croak,
Yet every note gives rise to hope!

The sun kicks back, it starts to sway,
A warm embrace at the end of day.
With each bright ray, a giggle flows,
Mother Nature joins the show; she knows!

So here's to laughter and all things grand,
In a concert hall of nature's hand.
With twirls and whirs, our spirits lift,
In this whimsical world, come share the gift!

Whirlpools of Wistful Whispers

Where secrets swirl like leaves in spin,
A rabbit grins, his mischief within.
Round and round the stories go,
Chasing dreams in soft-flowed glow.

The trees hold tales of bobbing hats,
While giggles echo from nearby chats.
A chipmunk pauses, thumbs in cheek,
His antics leave the breezes weak!

The moonlight winks through tangled hair,
As fireflies zip without a care.
In this woodland, we tumble and twist,
Nature's antics we can't resist!

So gather 'round, let laughter bloom,
In these whirlpools, there's always room.
For silly thoughts in twilight's gleam,
We dance along; it's all a dream!

Serendipity in the Sunbeams

By chance, I trip on a dandelion's dream,
It bursts apart, a fluffy scream.
With giggles echoing on lightly blown airs,
My shoes find wonders, oh, how it dares!

A ladybug struts, a tiny diva,
Winking green, she's quite the believer.
Beneath the branches, we twirl and spin,
As laughter bubbles, let the fun begin!

The shadows stretch and tease the ground,
In silly shapes, they leap around.
Every flower blooms with tales to share,
While daisies look on, quite unaware!

With rays of joy that never fade,
Dancing sunbeams form a merry parade.
So join me here for a whimsical spree,
In the treasure of chance, there's always glee!

The Calm of Nature's Conclave

In trees that dance with just a breeze,
Squirrels conspire, as they please,
A raucous crowd, in leafy halls,
Their giggles echo, nature calls.

A rabbit hops, a tale unfolds,
Of carrots lost, and legends bold,
The frogs all croak, they sing along,
Their chorus bursts, a comical throng.

The owl, a sage, with feathery grace,
Winks at the sun, with a wise old face,
While bugs in tuxedos boast and brawl,
A party hosted, beneath the sprawl.

The breeze it carries, mischief shared,
A potion mixed, oh how they dared,
And nature laughs, a cheery tune,
With every leaf and howling moon.

Retrospective Reverberations

The pond reflects a fishy grin,
As turtles toss their heads and spin,
A duck in boots, so dapper, dear,
Paddles past, with a quacky cheer.

Old trees recall with crackling bark,
The antics bright from dawn till dark,
The bunnies chased by blurry trains,
But giggles drown their little pains.

The sunbeams flicker, teasing smiles,
As ants march forth in fashionable styles,
A ladybug dons dots of red,
While all around them fun is spread.

A zephyr whispers tales of yore,
Of past adventures, laughs, and more,
In laughter's echo, nature plays,
A jesting world, through sunny rays.

Secrets Sheltered in the Shadows

The shadows dance, a hidden spree,
With secrets shared 'neath every tree,
A raccoon grins, plans a feast,
While whispers trot, and giggles crease.

The nightingale croons, a humorous plot,
Of scrapped up snacks that hit the spot,
While owls debate if moonlight's grand,
With friendly jests, a merry band.

Crickets chirp their nightly tune,
As fireflies blink, a lantern swoon,
The underbrush teems with absurd sights,
A snake who dances, oh what delights!

Through tangled vines and tangled feet,
The woodland jesters find their beat,
In rustling leaves, the laughter weaves,
A twinkling jest beneath the eaves.

An Invitation from the Interlaced Branches

In branches twine, a parley stands,
As whispers weave through leaf-bound strands,
The chipmunks scamper, woo-hoo, hooray!
Inviting all to join the play.

The wind it tickles every ear,
With tales of folly, loud and clear,
A hedgehog prances, spiky chic,
While dandelions giggle, so to speak.

A gathering blooms, the colors bright,
With buzzing bees in pure delight,
To celebrate the silliest feats,
As snickering blooms sway on their feet.

So find a nook, discover glee,
In frolic shared among the tree,
Where nature's jesters hum and sway,
An invite sent, come out and play!

Harmony in the Hidden Hollow

Beneath the boughs, the critters meet,
In silly dance with furry feet.
A squirrel spins, a rabbit hops,
The whole tree shakes as laughter tops.

The owl, with glasses, takes a look,
Judge of the antics, writes a book.
With every giggle, roots entwine,
In the hollow, all hearts align.

The chipmunk sings a plucky tune,
While bees buzz in a comical swoon.
The laughter lingers, sweet and bright,
In this woodland of pure delight.

As shadows stretch, the moon takes seat,
And woodland creatures count their treat.
A pie made of mushrooms, oak, and nuts,
Bring forth guffaws and little cuts!

Spirit Songs of the Forest Floor

On forest floor, the mushrooms sway,
As deer tell tales at the end of day.
A rabbit's joke, a fox's wink,
In every glance, the spirits blink.

A badger hums a silly tune,
While fireflies dance beneath the moon.
An acorn hat upon his head,
He jests of nuts gone to bed.

In hidden nooks where laughter flows,
A chatterbox of bouncing toes.
The ferns are swaying, green and tall,
With every jest, they're having a ball.

Mice gather round with tiny chairs,
As crickets strum without a care.
In this wild concert, joy takes flight,
Where spirit songs make hearts feel light.

Reveries Among the Rolling Roots

Amid the roots where laughter springs,
A bear performs his funny flings.
He juggles stones, oh what a sight,
As critters cheer with pure delight.

The hedgehog tells a tale so grand,
Of adventures close at hand.
While turtles trot with rhythmic grace,
In this whimsical woodland space.

With blossoms nodding to the beat,
Each joke becomes a tasty treat.
Laughter echoes through the trees,
On every breeze, a playful tease.

So join the dance, don't be shy,
Let your spirit soar and fly.
In rolling roots, the fun doesn't stop,
This merry romp, we cannot drop!

Sighs of the Solitary Stems

In quiet glades where stems reside,
A caterpillar giggles wide.
With secret jokes and silly puns,
He's the ruler of these fun runs.

The willow bends, it starts to sway,
As clouds above begin to play.
A drizzle drops, like giggles fall,
The forest answers the joyful call.

Beneath the stems, the shadows dance,
While mice engage in daring prance.
With twinkling eyes, they boldly dare,
To mimic flowers swaying rare.

The evening hums a gentle tune,
As laughter rises with the moon.
In every sigh among the trees,
Lies a world of fun and ease.

Serene Conversations with the Wind

The breeze tells jokes to the tall trees,
Leaves laugh softly, swaying with glee.
Squirrels debate what day it might be,
While birds chirp along, carefree as can be.

Sunlight giggles through branches so green,
Dancing shadows create a playful scene.
Even the flowers sway with delight,
As they join in on the teasing, so light.

A butterfly winks, flitting about,
Spinning tales of flowers, without a doubt.
The rustle of grass adds to the play,
Everything here feels like one grand ballet.

Nature's a comedian, bright and true,
In her audience, there's laughter anew.
With every rustle and murmured sound,
Joy is spilled in the grove all around.

Threads of Silence Among the Branches

In the grove where silence weaves a thread,
Each branch wears stories that giggle and spread.
The owls hoot softly, sharing a laugh,
While rabbits play tag, running in half.

A raccoon tells tales of a night so grand,
While the squirrels laugh, not a care in hand.
The shadows twist and turn in the light,
As whispers of joy make the day feel right.

Even the stillness is not without cheer,
With every creak, there's a chuckle to hear.
The moss is a carpet for secrets untold,
Under the trees, the laughter unfolds.

With a gentle breeze that tickles the ear,
Nature's comedy show is always near.
Every leaf holds a story that spins,
In the laughter of branches, real fun begins.

The Language of Leaves

The leaves are chattering, such a fine crew,
Speaking their language, old yet so new.
A dandelion giggles, swaying in place,
As a pine tree chuckles, keeping a face.

Maples gossip sweetly about the sun's rays,
While birches share tales of their silly ways.
In a flutter of petals, laughter takes flight,
As the garden rejoices in playful delight.

A breeze carries puns, carried far and wide,
And the roses blush pink, filled with great pride.
With every rustle, joy spills from the trees,
A comic performance that flows with the breeze.

Even the breeze plays a trick or two,
Tickling the flowers, in a dance just for you.
In the realm of leaves, humor is grand,
Printed in nature, like notes on a band.

Hushed Secrets of the Grove

In the grove, secrets giggle and sigh,
The bushes are blushing with dreams that fly.
A sneaky old fox shares a wink and a grin,
While the flowers perk up, ready to begin.

The trees lean close, to catch every word,
As whispers of mischief flutter and stirred.
The badger just chuckles, his belly aglow,
With mysteries shared that no one would know.

Amidst the soft whispers, there's laughter so sweet,
Nature's own comedy in each hidden feat.
The shadows play tricks, hiding all mirth,
In a world where each secret holds laughter's rebirth.

The air is delicious with jests yet untold,
Stories are woven like threads spun from gold.
With each rustle, the giggles collide,
In the hush of the grove, where joy can't hide.

The Soundtrack of Sylvan Solitude

In the woods where squirrels dance,
The trees hum tunes of chance.
Birds gossip in sweet refrain,
While rabbits join in the silly train.

Leaves rustle, a secret shared,
With every twig, nature's dared.
The wind giggles, a playful breeze,
Tickling the branches with perfect ease.

Mice hold a wild karaoke night,
Singing songs 'til morning light.
Even deer sway to the beat,
As crickets keep the perfect heat.

Oh, the symphony of the glade,
Where laughter and joy never fade.
Join the fun, in this leafy show,
In the woodland's heart, come and glow!

Echoes of the Enclosed Eden

In a garden where gnomes get fancy,
Bouncing about like they're in a chancy.
Flowers nodding their heads in delight,
As bees buzz by with all their might.

Bunnies hopping with zest and flair,
Swapping tales with the nearest hare.
The sun winks down with a bright smile,
As ladybugs strut, living in style.

Frogs croak in a chorus sublime,
Challenging the crickets to keep up with time.
Underneath a dappled sky,
The whole garden seems to sigh.

Oh, the echoes in this vibrant space,
Where every creature finds their place.
Join the laughter, share the cheer,
In this Eden, joy is near!

Heartbeats of Hidden Habitats

In the thicket where shadows play,
Tiny critters have their say.
With acorns flying left and right,
Join the ruckus, it's quite a sight!

Hedgehogs rolling like fluffy balls,
Making mischief as nature calls.
Turtles taking their slow parade,
While foxes strike a pose that's made.

The chorus of chirps, such sweet delight,
Even slugs groove under the pale moonlight.
Every heartbeat in this lovely maze,
Tells stories of whimsical, funny days.

So gather round, lend your ear,
To the unseen joy lurking near.
In hidden habitats, laughter resides,
Where the heart of nature abides!

The Poetry of Pattering Petals

In gardens where petals patter and glide,
Butterflies twirl, with nothing to hide.
Bees buzz in their patterned suit,
While ants march in perfect pursuit.

Every bloom has a secret to share,
Fluttering in the sunlight's glare.
Daisies giggle, a playful sight,
Competing in color, joy, and light.

Underneath the big oak's embrace,
The shadows dance, setting the pace.
Grasshoppers sing with a jolly tune,
Under the watchful eye of the moon.

Oh, the poetry flows on this ground,
With soft whispers and laughter abound.
Join the ballet of petals and cheer,
In this garden, happiness is near!

Voices Among the Vines

In the tangled vines, secrets crawl,
They debate on who's the funniest of all.
A grape told a joke, the fig cracked a grin,
While the banana slipped, causing giggles to begin.

Laughter dances, like shadows they play,
The peas burst out jokes, brightening the gray.
A leaf fell down, it claimed it could float,
While a sneaky little beetle said, 'I am a boat!'

Beneath the sun, their chatter rings clear,
As one little berry sings, 'Let's all have a cheer!'
With puns on the breeze, and a tickle of air,
These playful little fruits hang light as a prayer.

Bouncing about, from vine to vine,
They roll in the dirt, feeling just fine.
A cherry said, "Life is just like a joke,
You never know when it's ripe for a poke!"

Serenity in the Shaded Glade

In the glade so serene, a squirrel takes a nap,
While the ants host a show in a leaf-made cap.
Grasshoppers chirp, unknowingly absurd,
Competing for laughs, though silence is heard.

The mushrooms giggle, all spotted and bright,
Sharing tales of the wind, what a funny sight!
A shroom smirks, "I'm quite a fungi,
You'll laugh till you cry, just give me a try!"

Beneath leafy branches, a parade is on,
Of critters who dance till the early dawn.
The laughter erupts as a twig trips a toad,
In this shady retreat, all worries erode.

So gather 'round friends, let's munch on some cheer,
Join in this merry, whimsical sphere.
Life's just a jest, under this leafy lair,
In this glade of laughter, there's magic to spare!

Beneath the Gentle Canopy

Beneath the soft leaves, a fox starts to yawn,
As turtles on logs sing the day's funny song.
A raccoon drops by with a wig made of grass,
Saying, "Look at me now, I've got style and sass!"

The quails kick a ball made of fluff and twine,
While a wise old owl claims he's danced with a vine.
The shadows are cheeky, they tickle and tease,
As the branches above sway, just like a breeze.

A flower pipes up, with petals so bright,
"I can wiggle and giggle, just hold me tight!"
With worms doing limbo in dirt so divine,
This gathering's antics are simply sublime.

So come take a seat, on this soft, cozy floor,
You'll laugh till you ache, and then laugh some more.
In this canopy world, where the silly hold sway,
Every chuckle and giggle brightens the day!

The Rustling of the Resting Trees

The trees start to rustle, awake from their dreams,
A wise old oak whispers, "Life's not as it seems!"
The birch has a punchline, oh don't let it miss,
While the pines giggle soft, "We're just sharing bliss!"

A squirrel declares, with a flair for the jest,
"I don't mean to brag, but I acorn the best!"
All the branches shake gleefully, tickled by air,
As each tree tells a tale, laughter everywhere.

The leaves wave hello, with a chuckle and cheer,
"Who knew ancient wisdom could tickle like beer?"
Funny little critters come out for the show,
With jokes so corny, they'd make popcorn glow!

So listen dear friends, to this forest of fun,
Where everything's goofy, no need to outrun.
In the rustling of trees, the humor runs free,
It's a laugh in the woods, just come and see!

www.ingramcontent.com/pod-product-compliance
Lightning Source LLC
Chambersburg PA
CBHW071838160426
43209CB00003B/343